Night of the Chickens

Written by Danny Pearson

Illustrated by César Samaniego

Collins

1 Light of the moon

One night, by the light of the moon, drops of rain fell.

plop, plop

There was a flash of lightning.

Toad was asleep.

splash

He sat up with a fright.

What was that splash?

In the moonlight, Toad spotted chickens in his pool.

splash

Yak had a peek. There were sixteen chickens looking back at him.

Moo!

All of a sudden, the chickens took flight.

2 We need help!

Toad, Yak, Pug and Bat had a meeting.

The chickens do not look right!

3 Look!

Goat lost the book. He was livid.

19

There was a flash of lightning.

Chickens, you are free!

flash

The chickens took off for freedom.

The end.

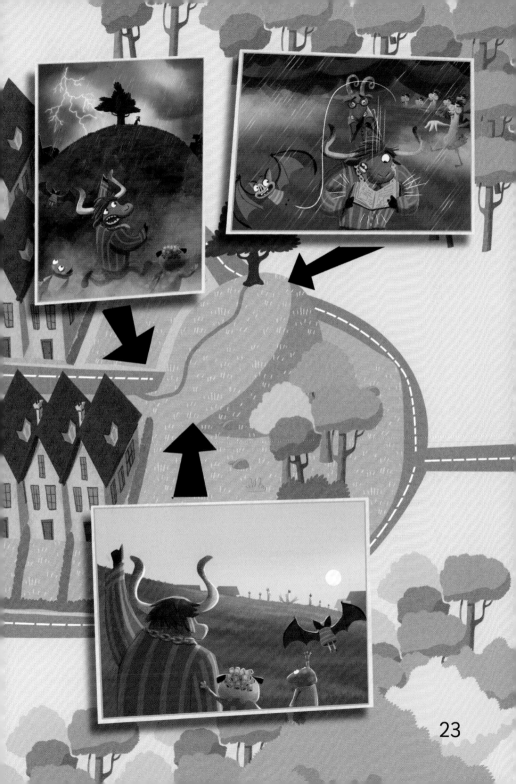

After reading

Letters and Sounds: Phases 3 and 4

Word count: 226

Focus phonemes: /ch/ /sh/ /th/ /ng/ /ai/ /ee/ /igh/ /oa/ /oo/ /oo/, and adjacent consonants

Common exception words: of, to, the, no, I, into, all, by, are, he, we, me, was, you, they, do, come, were, there, one, out, what, her

Curriculum links: Science – Animals, including humans

National Curriculum learning objectives: Reading/word reading: apply phonic knowledge and skills as the route to decode words; read accurately by blending sounds in unfamiliar words containing GPCs that have been taught; Reading/comprehension (KS2): understand what they read, in books they can read independently, by checking that the text makes sense to them, discussing their understanding and explaining the meaning of words in context; discussing words and phrases that capture the reader's interest and imagination

Developing fluency

- Demonstrate reading a page with expression and drama.
- Encourage your child to read every other page, using different voices for characters and reading sound and action words with emphasis.

Phonic practice

- Turn to page 4 and point to **splash**. Encourage your child to sound out each letter or letter pair and blend.
- Challenge them to read the following words that have more than one consonant at the beginning:
  fright   spotted   flash   free
- Challenge your child to read the following two syllable words. Can they identify the syllables in each?
  freedom   livid   chickens   peckish   sixteen

Extending vocabulary

- Turn to page 9 and point to **quick as a flash**. Discuss its meaning. (e.g. *very fast, speedily*)
- Point to the chickens' eyes on page 8 and say: "The eyes are as big as saucers." Take turns to choose a detail in a picture and describe it using "as". (e.g. page 21: *chickens are as fast as motorbikes*)